MOURNING JEWELRY

Stephanie M. Wytovich

RAW DOG
SCREAMING
PRESS

Mourning Jewelry © 2014 by Stephanie M. Wytovich

Previously published:
Pear Tree Press. Slyvia and Vows: Vicious Oral Whims of Speech. Print 2013.
Cellar Door: Words of Beauty Tales of Terror. James Ward Kirk Publishing.
"Hide and Seek." Print 2013.
Bones. James Ward Kirk Publishing. "Calcium." Print 2013.
The Wicked Library. "The Primrose Path," Sylvia, and Vows: Vicious Oral
Whims of Speech. Audio, 2012-13.
The Horror Zine. "Blackness" and "Succubus." 2013.
Jamais Vu-Journal of Strange Among the Familiar. "Ballet of Knives," and
"Eventually, You Become Immune." Post Mortem Press. Print. 2014

Published by Raw Dog Screaming Press
Bowie, MD

First Edition

Cover illustration: Steven Archer
Cover design: Jennifer Barnes
Book design: M. Garrow Bourke

ISBN 978-1-935738-63-3
Library of Congress Control Number: 2014939149

Printed in the United States of America

www.RawDogScreaming.com

CONTENTS

Dedication

For September, for June

Author's Note

THERE IS SOMETHING quite intoxicating about losing someone, even if that someone is yourself. In some ways it's a release of pain, while in others, it's an acceptance, a welcoming of the emptiness. I've always found great pleasure playing with darkness, and between these pages, there are characters and creatures that thrive on absence, that breed in tears. *Mourning Jewelry* is a collection about the haunted, about memories that can't be escaped, and despite my best efforts, there just never seemed to be enough poison to quiet the shadows on the walls.

And so I wrote, wrote and met entities and beings that lived in a plane, in a realm that is not our own. Mourning was a muse who walked me through the cemetery, who introduced me to the energy of the mausoleum, and who dug graves and exhumed stories about women who learned about ghosts—who experienced obsession—in ways that gave new blood to my nightmares, new flesh to my prose.

To me, the concept of mourning jewelry is not something that you wear around your neck. It's not a locket or a ring. It's a sickness, a sadness, and it's something that you carry around with you, inside of you. It's a disease that wears on your body like dried tears on lace, an invisible stain like blood on twice-bleached bed sheets. *Mourning Jewelry* is the knife against the wedding dress and the black veil caught in the tree branch. It's the thunder at dawn and the draft in your bedroom at three a.m.

But make no mistake. These are not weak women, not tired little girls. Some of the best madness is within those who know that they have nothing left to lose. After all, everyone mourns, but not everyone cries.

—*Stephanie M. Wytovich*

A Match Made by the Devil

He was a touch of wicked.
She was a shot of whiskey.
He liked to spar.
She liked to burn.
And when they met,
the world blacked out.
The night started to spin.
Hearts started to fall.
Because he was a pinch of danger.
and she was pint of Hell.

Airless

Suffocation would be a reprieve
from the taunting image of
the face that lingers in my
memory like mist on a cold
autumn morning

I wish my breath would
cease to flow in these weary
tubes that lead to crushed lungs,
abandoned by a broken heart
that has packed its suitcase
but can't seem to leave the
comfort of hurt it's lodged itself in

When I gag, I smile, hoping that
the air will purge itself from my
chest—that I can throw up the pain—
vomit the remembrance of years passed,
of tears cried, of scars born

Yes, suffocation would be a blessing
from a world where each breath
I take, reminds me that I'm alone,
that the life I lived was a lie,
and that the person that I loved was nothing
more than a foul gust of air that
moved through a hollow woman
filled with too much want

As I Sit and Wonder

Do I love you?
Of course not, but that doesn't mean
that I don't care for you, that I don't
pine for you like a schoolgirl when you're gone.
And even though my heart didn't break when you left,
it did crack, a small line right down the middle
where it bled—and continues to bleed—to this
very moment. No, it's not love, but it is something,
and that something is painful, and I wish it would stop.

Asphyxiation

Strangle me,
wrap your hands around my neck
shove your voice down
my throat;
Let my tongue wrap up
your apology
and gag on your lies

God, I like the silence
So

Choke me again,
rip out my esophagus
make me mute, still,
because this is better
than deceit;
Asphyxiation is
a permanent promise

Ballet of Knives

She eased the knives out of the drawer and waved them
through the air as if they were multi-colored
ribbons in a dance routine. Her ballet was soft, filled
with monotone twirls and a light passé, and when she scraped the blades
against the walls, she did so in a delicate pirouette, leaving
scratch marks in the paper while the blur of her black
leotard moved before an audience that was no longer there.

This time I'll dance the blood ballet.
This time, I'll nail it.

The knives were her people now, those long, silver sticks of
metal that dove through the air and sliced failure like a practiced
balancoire. She worshipped them, performed for them, and when she
made a mistake—when she tripped or stumbled, fell or went out
of position—she cut a thin, one-inch line into her thigh as a
reminder that perfection isn't an option. It's a necessity. Especially
when dancing in blood.

Blackness

It came to me screaming,
smothering its children like
post-partum mothers drowning
their sorrows in fresh
baptism two days after birth

I cringed at the minor-key
siren song it wailed in the
ink-spattered sky, poisoning
my eardrums with an inviting
brutality that blanketed
me in suffocation and
stabbed at my heart song

I could not breathe,
the color ate away at my throat
devouring what happiness
remained in this flesh husk,
and my body, desperate to survive,
purged the venom but
continued to build up the shadows
that pooled at my feet,
dragging me further into the
guttural cry that claimed me
the moment I closed my eyes

Bloodletting

There are little cuts of sadness
that bleed from my arms—punishment
for every time I think of him. I never
see the knife, but I always feel it, and I
imagine that it's sterling silver, adorned
with a Corinthian rose handle, the one he
used to open my letters with. I pretend he's
merely writing me love notes to wake up to,
careful calligraphy strung together by the
heart of a romantic, but I know that I'm
the poet because I always sign my work.

Calcium

My place is with the ashes,
in yesterday's promises
and today's regrets. I don't pretend
that I belong here—that I'm something other
than what I am—but I spread my wings
and stretch out my claws, the Devil's grin
on an angel's face.

Their bones are around me,
swaddled in last week's flesh,
soaked and boiled in blood
just the way I like it. I don't pretend
that I belong here—that I'm something other
than what I am—but I eat men
and torture hearts until they break, wait until
they peel off their flesh to get away
from my touch.

And then I use their femurs like toothpicks,
crack open their pallor shells
and suck out the marrow like
Bergamot tea. I don't pretend
that I belong here—that I'm something other
than what I am—but the calcium
keeps me alive, stirring in the corners
as I wait for your skeleton and thrive
in the remains of last lover's kill.

Charon's Assistant

I put the coin in his mouth.
I swear it! I did exactly as you told me to.
But no matter where I placed it, or how many
coins I used, they disintegrated on his tongue,
bubbling and boiling on his taste buds as if I'd
poured acid down the old man's throat. It wasn't
my fault. I tried to make payment, tried to send
in my dues, but his body wouldn't take it, it kept
spitting them out, vomiting the leftover mush
in my face, on my shirt. Maybe he's afraid of boats?
Maybe he's already seasick? But he refuses to get
onboard.

No, you must me joking.
You can't be serious!

What do you mean I have to take him? That
he's my responsibility now? What am I supposed
to do with the body? With the soul? Should I just
chop him up and put him in a treasure chest of
silver and gold? Hope that one day he swallows
a piece of eight and makes his way back to you? I
don't want to be a body collector, a harbinger
of souls. That's why I'm the assistant! The messenger!
Tell me, Charon, what's a young girl supposed to do
with a rotted corpse on her hands? Especially one
that keeps her up at night and won't stop screaming…

Consistent, Yet Deadly

When she hurts, when she aches, when she pains,
she kills. And only then. No exceptions, no ands,
ifs, or buts. But she's always hurting, always aching,
always in pain. And so she's always killing, always
subtracting, always taking. But she knows no better,
and cares not for what she does. Murdering is in her
blood. As is a constant state of mourning.

Corpse Flower

GRAB A SHOVEL. THE DIRT is soft, but you can never be too sure with these things. And I like to be sure. That's why I asked you here, tonight. The anniversary of the night it all began. The night I first saw her after it all—the beautiful corpse flower that popped out of the ground, adorned in white lace, face peppered with mud with bits of crunched up roses in her hair. She smelled like lavender, a soft aroma with a hint of honeysuckle, and she moved with the grace of a firefly searching for her mate. She was beautiful, and I couldn't take my eyes off her, no matter how heavy the air made my heart, no matter the sadness that dripped off her dress like teardrops in the two o'clock hour. I wanted to call to her, to remind her, to forgive her. But I couldn't. I just stood there, hidden in the shadows, watching her while she looked for me.

Once every ten years, she wakes up and blooms, spreads her arms and stretches out her legs, takes a midnight stroll through the forest and dances with the gentle sway of the trees. A nighttime ballerina, she moves and loses herself in the raven's song, a dark duet with the blackbirds that trail her like children afraid of getting lost. She's their mother and they wait for her, cry for her, mourn with her for she's not the only one that's lost someone.

I hide from them, too.

Are you still listening? Because it's almost time and she only lives for 48 hours. And after 60 years of watching, of wishing, of praying, I'm ready to forgive her, to go to her, but my body no longer can. I can't dance with her like we used to, can't twirl her, dip her, hold her…and I know that even though she won't show it, that even though she'd pretend it was the ideal reunion, that she'd be disappointed in the lines on my face, with the bags under my eyes, the way my legs hang dead and lifeless in this chair, and the way the machine manages my breath. You see, we were kids when we married, and we acted like two fools in love, living fast and reckless until the moment she stopped breathing. What we had was fire, and I never forgave her for leaving me. That's why she comes back. And that's why I can't forgive myself.

So I want you to go to her. Make sure it's easy for her to wake up and that the ground is dry and soft so it doesn't stick to her face or her dress. I want you to dance with her like I can't and tell her that she blooms brighter, fuller, and more beautiful than any flower in this town. Go ahead, take the shovel. I want tonight to be perfect for her. I want her to feel alive, to dance, to sing, to be with a man that makes her feel like a woman. I want her to be at peace but more than anything, I want her to stop looking, to stop searching. I want her to move on and rest easy.

Just tell her that I'm sorry.

That I'm so, so sorry.

Daddy's Little Grave Digger

I've hated the sight of a shovel since I've been
six years old. Dad used to make me carry it out
to the woods above my head, holding it high as if
it was some trophy I should be privileged to hold,
and I guess after all these years, it kind of ended up
being one. A trophy of sorts. Just not the kind
you're probably used to.

See, Dad had a bad back so I was in charge of
maintenance. I'd scope out the land, dig the holes,
and chuck the bodies in their graves and cover them
up before anyone knew they were even missing. I was
the little girl who made dirt blankets, the girl who fashioned
funeral clothes out of leaves and twigs, and the child who left
markings on the trees so she could remember who went where.
I was Daddy's little girl. Daddy's little grave digger, and some
things never change. Old habits die hard, and now I'm digging
for myself, hopefully making the old man proud as he looks up
at me from the hole I dug especially for him, six feet down
into the earth.

Dare I Keep the Body

The first time I saw a dead body, I wanted to keep it,
to hold it close and never let it out of my sight. It was
the most alive thing that I'd ever encountered and after
years of feeling stagnant, of feeling stuck, I finally came
back to life with the simple sight of his glazed-over eyes.
So I took him. I dragged him out to my car and placed his
corpse in my backseat and drove home as if it was just a pile of
groceries back there, as if it was a bad egg that soured the smell
and not the stench of his rotted flesh.

But then I couldn't leave him.
I wanted him with me everywhere I went, so I cut off one of
his thumbs and stuck it in my jacket pocket. I'd finger it
sometimes—scratch and pick at the nail when I got bored—but
then I wanted more of him with me, on me. I took a chunk of his hair
and put it in my locket so it hung down next to my heart. I yanked out
one of his molars and sucked on the tooth when I missed his taste.
And when I really needed my fix, when I knew I couldn't be without
his touch all day, I'd sew a patch of his skin inside my bra
so I could feel him on me, always close, always near. It may
not have been a conventional romance, but our relationship thrived
until he withered away, decomposing like a banana peel in my backyard.
I buried him, along with my dirty secret, under the flowerbeds, and now
I smile every time I pick a rose. The girls in my office love them. They say
they bring the place back to life.

Death Has its Own Angels

There wasn't the slightest hesitation
when she pushed the pillow to his face.
In fact, she quite liked the way the feathers
exploded out the sides—poof!—and showered
them both in a bath of white. They would have
matched her own wings if she'd have gone up—
ascended to the pearly gates instead of the black
castle below. But here she was, done up in wings
that smelled of brimstone and swarmed with flies,
wings that whispered *things* she didn't want to hear,
didn't want to do—but she did them anyways. And
sometimes she enjoyed it, especially when she got
to kiss the victims and take their dying breath.

Drown Your Sorrows

I used to think happiness was a glass of cheap champagne
and a night in your arms;
I didn't need much,
I just needed you.

But now that champagne is top-shelf whiskey
chased with nights of regret;
And now I need the bottle
since I can no longer have you.

End of the Line

I don't care that you're not ready.
Time's up. Put on your sad face.
It's time to die.

Eventually, You Become Immune

At first it was only one cup a night. I'd boil the water
until the tea kettle screamed, pour it in my favorite red
mug, and test the temperature with the tip of my tongue.
Hot. Ouch. Ooh. I wanted it to burn, and it was only after
I couldn't taste anything that I threw in the herbs. I didn't
wait for them to bleed, didn't wait for them to clump together
so I could strain them out. No. I watched them hover on the
top like bloated bodies, and when they started to sink, I closed
my eyes and swallowed them whole.

And then it was two cups a night. Two cups of herbs,
two mouthfuls of bodies. I tried to change flavors
but I liked the way the spice and cloves rolled over my
senses and nipped at the back of my throat. So I made another
cup, this time, with even more herbs, more bodies. And
by the end of the night, I was drunk on death, bloated and face
down in the bathtub, my spirit overlooking my corpse.

I shook my head and reached for the mug. Even now, I wanted
a steaming cup of bodies, but there weren't any herbs left in
the cupboards. No honeysuckle, rosebay, gelsemium. The hemlock
was empty. The jar for nightshade dry. Three cups of tea,
three mouthfuls of bodies. How had I survived that long?

Everyone's Doing it

Peer pressure is a bitch, especially
when you die. I didn't want to drink
the wine, but they—the women in black—said
that I should, that it would change my life and
that the world as I knew it would never be the same:
no more sadness, no more heartbreak, no more same
old, same old, every single day. They just left out the
part where it stopped my heart from beating,
where their blood—the sweet merlot that I thought
I was drinking—took over mine and drained my years,
stole my youth. But look on the positive side, now I'm
in with the dead crowd, and no one says no to corpse.

Exception #1

There are no exceptions.
Everyone dies: some when I tell them to,
Others when I don't.

Falling, Rising into Love

He asked me if I wanted to fall back in love, and very honestly, I told him no. That I'm sick of falling in love, of falling into bed, of falling into graves. I'm tired of having to pick myself up and walk on broken promises, empty promises. I'm exhausted from falling, from tripping into love, collapsing into graves. The stumble isn't worth it. The stagger too much pain. I limp from falling in love. I bleed from subsiding to love. But ascending to love…that's beauty beyond the veil. For if you asked me to climb into your heart, to take my time with your heart, then I would walk journeys to calm the storm in your eyes. I would clear mountains and swim rivers to be with you, to love you. I would scale time, fight age, and battle death if you wanted me to ascend to love, to grow to love, to develop, breed, and nurture love. But I will not *fall* in love. No. I will only rise from the grave for it.

Fireflies Dance for the Souls of Heroes

The children sat in a circle waiting for the sun
to disappear, to creep beneath the trees and bow
down to the moon. The ground was wet, and it sank
through their threadbare jeans, chilling their innocent
flesh while the fire bugs bred around their feet. The fireflies
needed youth, craved the naïvety of a child, and they
hypnotized them with their glowing bodies, with their
playful dance. The children would sing, would praise
their lightning gods, and the fireflies would grow stronger
as they summoned the souls of heroes in the wind, drawing
them in with their light so they could have the chance,
the opportunity to live again in the night.

Free my Soul

I saw myself hanging limp in his arms, strung out and damp
like a load of wrinkled, wet laundry not yet held out to dry. My
soul was a mix of colors—silver, beige, and blue—and I wondered
if some of my flesh tones had actually bled into the mix when
he washed away my life.

I don't like how he holds me. There's no balance or symmetry to
the position I'm in, and it looks as if at any given moment that I'm going
to slide down his arms and fall into the shadows. I wish someone
would help me, but everyone here turns their heads and refuses to
make eye contact with me. They don't want to believe that it's
possible, that someone like me could be with someone like him,
but here I am, trapped in the Devil's embrace, and no one can
hear me scream.

Frozen Eyes

There's ice in my eyes,
a hailstorm
that rains down on me
freezing what I see—
what I thought
I saw—
what I still believe
is there,
but know isn't
for it she he and they
watch me while I sleep
as I thrash in the storm,
cold and restless
as I dream of their
winter stare

Garden of Karma

The flowers die where she walks
and nothing she plants will ever grow,
for the soil is tainted with blood and
decomposed flesh, and the man beneath
it eats all of her seeds.

Garlic Hangs Above Her Bed

She nailed the wreath to her headboard
and drove a wooden stake through the
middle as a warning to the man that
would visit her that night. She wove roses
around the cloves of garlic to help with
the smell and to catch the blood that fell
from the Christ impostor's wounds. She
wasn't fooled by the presence of the halo,
for she could smell ash and sulfur on his
breath and no amount of darkness could
hide the two fangs that slid out his mouth
when he looked in at her from her
bedroom window.

Gravestones for Breakfast

Every morning at the break of dawn
she goes to her personal cemetery in
her backyard, and breaks off a piece
of the cement blocks she uses as markers
for her three recently departed husbands,
all tragically dead from what the doctors thought
were *natural causes*. But there's nothing natural
about death when it's shoved down your throat
when you're asleep at night and now when she
takes her coffee in the morning, she does so with
cream and a pinch of sugar and headstone
to liven up the taste.

Grieving in Diamonds

Her tears, they dripped from her eyes like
crystal balls, thick as glass and filled with
secrets. She wasn't sad he was dead, wasn't
even troubled, but she cried like the saddest
of wives, mourned like the grieving widow
she should have been. And people believed her.
They bought the charades, apologized for the mask
of grief she wore so well, but inside she was
laughing.

They are all
so stupid

But still her tears fell like rain, blotting out her
cherry red lipstick and sending streams of
mascara down her face. She played the part well,
knew how to stumble when she walked, how to
scream when the music hit the right note, when to
faint when it all became too much. She was a practiced
woman and the routine was always the same. And they
always fell for it, always. So she played up the theatrics,
gave the performance, the story, of a woman with a broken
heart, and then when they were gone, when everyone had
left, she laughed—really let herself laugh—all the way to
the bank.

Haunted By the Thought of You

I close my eyes, but not before
I've checked the locks—once, twice, three times—
just to make sure, and even then, I sleep halfway
between dreams and nightmares, afraid that you'll
appear in my hallway, covered in soot, in ash,
and make me pay for what I did, and what I
don't regret doing.

He Likes to Watch

At first when I slept with him, I felt shame. There was something not
okay about being with another man so soon after it happened, but yet
there I was, laying on top of him, drawn to him like flies to death.
I smiled when I touched him, even though inside I was dying,
coming apart at the seams, my veins unwinding, my organs shutting
down. I wanted to feel whole, wanted to feel *something,* but no matter
how many times I bedded him, not matter how many orgasms I faked,
I was still alone, still without the man that I'd buried six feet deep
this time last week. And so the other man, the man that was not my husband,
the man that was not the one in the ground, asked me what was wrong, why
I kept staring at the corner. And I told him—yes, I told him!—that you were there.
You, the corpse of my late spouse, standing there, watching me, watching him,
watching us. And I knew that you wouldn't leave. That you'd stay there and
haunt me every time I opened my heart, every time I spread my legs. Every kiss,
every hug, every fuck, you'd be there. Always watching, always part of the act.
An ever-present threesome every time I closed my eyes.

Hide and Seek

There's a cellar door in my head—
an empty room filled with cobwebs
and lost souls—one that I try to visit
when I climb into bed at night,
scare myself to sleep.

A montage of pictures flash behind
sleepy eyes as old faces and forgotten places—
dog-eared memories, yellowed and frayed—
crawl out of the darkness and into the dusty
musk that floods my head.

I see behind the closed doors,
collect monsters and nightmares
in mason jars, and when the cold
embraces me—wraps me in its secrets—
I smile at the whispers from the voices
that can't stay buried, laugh in the dark
at the handprints on the walls,
and when I follow the footsteps…
I hear them behind me.

They live in the forgotten, the grey area
where baptism fails, where they thrive
in the impossible—floating on broken
legs with cut heels, their necks snapped
and limp on their shoulders—and when I open that
cellar door in my head, the bad dreams
become real, the things that lurk underneath

wooden floorboards surface,
and madness comes out to play for one more
round of Hide and Seek.

His Kiss Brought Corpses

She didn't close her eyes
the second time she kissed him.
He tasted like serpents
and she wanted to see the venom,
wanted to feel the spell.
So she took his hand in hers
and they danced,
danced and kissed until the city lights went out,
until the corpses started to rise,
and then they danced some more
kissed some more,
drunk off each other's laughter,
high off the scent of voodoo in the air.

I Do

He doesn't know that I did it—and neither does anyone else—so
you'll have to promise me that you'll keep my secret. Truth be told,
we don't even speak anymore, it's like we're miles apart when in reality
we can't take more than three steps away from each other or else
the pain starts to reverberate through both of our bodies.

I just wanted him to be mine
I didn't want him to leave

But spells have a way of backfiring when your intentions
aren't clear, so when I plucked those couple of hairs from his
head and wove them into my braid, the words that I said did
not match the feelings that I felt, and emotions are so much more
than just bottled up secrets that we pretend our heart likes to keep
from our brain. They are portals and charms and they bound him
to me that night, bound him physically, but not emotionally.

And now when I walk, I pull him along with an invisible leash
and he follows like a beaten puppy dog afraid of his master. There's
no love or admiration, there's only hatred and spite, and I can't take
the braid out, can't release him from my hold, and when I try to
reverse the spell—and I try, I try!—all I hear is laughter. Laughter
and wedding bells.

If You Look for Me, You Won't Find Me

When he died—at least I think he died—I felt a coldness surround me, almost as if my entire body was covered in snowflakes. I don't remember burying him, so maybe he's not dead, maybe he just left, or went away... perhaps he disappeared into the same chilled air that hugs me in his absence, that strangles me with memories of his touch. I wonder where he's at, wonder what he's doing, and sometimes, I even look for him. But there's no use. There are times in life when you can't find someone—no matter how hard you search for them—if they don't want to be found.

Into the Fade

Sometimes when I close my eyes,
I see you die.
It's a slow death where you fade
away from me,
a static absence between the pages
where I used to write
down your name.

I don't always cry
but sometimes I die a little.
It's an ache that buries memories
inside my chest,
a nest for pain that burrows
into the heart
that used to pump
for you.

It's hard to forget
when your face is plastered
everywhere I look
because for so long,
my eyes saw only you
and now when I close them,
I see you die,
but not because you're dead,
but because you're not
here anymore.

It Happened in the City

Her whisper smelled like bourbon,
and when he kissed her, he got drunk off her lips.
It happened fast—too fast, maybe—and before either
of them knew what was happening, they were lost
in each other's arms with no worries, no responsibilities,
and no obligations. For a brief moment in time, there
was nothing but them, just city lights, empty drinks
and the hope that when it was over, that when it was all said and done,
that they would find their way back,
back to the city, back to the moment
somehow, someway, for one more night.

It was Hunger

And we were in love in lust and I kissed her, oh did I kiss her, and I wanted her, needed her I wrapped her legs around my neck, dove into the wet diamond of her femininity, my hair tracing circles on her milk white thighs as I left crimson kisses on her flesh, it was sublime, it was ecstasy and I was cutting and tearing, biting listening to her scream, and she came in waves of blood and I drank it up like the wine it was, cherry red and sweet as I ate her from the outside in.

I Wish Mother Wouldn't Cry

She wasn't always terrible. Sometimes, she cried.
It didn't happen often, but there were those rare
occasions when she'd break down. But even then,
she didn't just cry. She thrashed around the house,
threw dishes against the wall, broke cups with her
fists and then ripped out the glass shards in her skin with
her teeth. She'd spit them at me, her mouth bloodied,
her lips curled in a snarl. I'd run away, lock myself
in my room, away from her, away from the beast she
became when she grew sad. I preferred when she was
terrible, when she was awful because then I wasn't scared,
because then I knew what to expect. It was when she
cried that I got worried. It was when the tears came that
I knew I had to hide.

Jade Keeps the Rot Away

It wouldn't be a problem if she didn't smell so much, but I
think people are starting to wonder what the odor coming from
underneath my bed is about. I wrapped her in gauze, stuffed bits
of jade in her nose, mouth, eyes, and ears and prayed over her
bloody stumps that she'd stop decomposing, stop rotting away. I wasn't
ready for her to leave me yet. We still had things to talk about and
she needed to stop running away.

Jasper, Name Him Jasper

The baby pushed, clawed, screamed, and cried,
its eyes shown red and
pouring blood.

Make it stop
Make it stop

The women pushed, clawed, screamed and cried,
The jasper clutched in her hand,
pouring blood.

He's coming
He's coming

They pushed, clawed, screamed, and cried,
both their pain gone,
along with both of their lives.

Key to Heaven, Key to Hell

St. Peter looked at her, his eyes narrow and wet as
he fingered the key in his hands, nervous for her
soul. It would be Heaven, or it would be Hell, and there
was no saying which because forgiveness could only
get her so far as her heart was full of sin, and her
wings were already clipped from her back—*pray for me*—and
she fell, disappeared in the fires, walked through
the ice, and St. Peter knew that he would never see
her again, that she would never fly back to him because
the decision was final, and she accepted it with a smile.

Kiss My Soul to Sleep

Every time he kisses me, I die a little more, and it feels
like butterfly wings against my chest, like warm milk dribbling
down my chin and it fills me full with the sweetest of agonies
as I pull him closer, kiss him deeper, swallowing this saliva of
death that I crave every morning at the break of dawn.

Knot Undone

He stopped breathing
and I couldn't
stop
watching,
couldn't stop
untying the knot
piece after piece,
undoing
his
life.

Let it Pour

I heard you like the sound of rain.
So think of me when you hear the thunder:
loud, screaming, threatening. I want your heart
to drop when you hear me coming, when I
come, and after I came.

Leviathan Swallows the Sun

Unconscious in the dark blue waters,
Leviathan remains asleep, waiting for her voice to
awaken him, to chant him back to life. Every nine
months she cries as her children start to die, so
she calls to him to open the skies to
primeval chaos, to birth the fertility
rain as he swallows the sun and brings in the storm
of the sea. She lights her candles—white, red, and
green—and casts her spell in the eclipse, praying
to the monster—the very serpent that swam inside her
and laid his eggs in her womb—that her babies
would live to see another year, that the pain of death
would stop hurting, and that the unborn children
would stop trying to claw their way out of her—ripping
her skin, her womanhood, and her heart—in desperation
to get back to him.

Loving a Man Like That

Nothing will help you with a man like that. You can trust me. I know how he walks, how he moves through life, through people, and when a man like that whispers words with a poet's tongue, with a serpent's tongue, there is nothing for a woman to do but let down her veil and prepare her heart, for those words are nothing but poison—no matter how sweet they taste—and no matter how tempting he is in the beginning, eventually he will kill you. Oh yes, I can promise you that.

Lullaby

Tears on glass
like raindrops after a thunderstorm
leak through the cracks,
the broken shards
that prick my cheeks as I stick
my face through the window,
desperate for a glimpse of the outside world,
a world where blood doesn't flow
so steady from my veins,
where regret doesn't fall like sadness
on my pillowcase

Midnight Confessions of an Ex-Virgin

When the stars came out
and the lies started to spill, the boy looked
at the girl, and the girl stared at the ground,
ashamed, embarrassed, as her purity—
what she used to be known for—slid down her legs
in wet tentacles that dripped lust and perversion
into small puddles that reflected what used to be
her virginity as it died kicking and screaming on the forest floor.

Mother Moon

She is an evil temptress, a wanton soul that hangs above me—
in front of me, behind me—constantly whispering in my ear,
telling me about the secrets that hide underneath shadows and
the gossip that breeds behind stars. She fantasizes about lovers,
about unholy affairs and she expects me to join her, to fly by her
side and sit with her while she laughs and watches them,
manipulates them with her astrological pull. But she does not own
me like she owns them, for I am immune to her hypnosis, her
silver-studded charm. Born out of wedlock, the constellations
are my fathers, and my mother is a mistress, but she is *not* my keeper
for I am no one's possession, and I refuse to be owned by either moon
or star.

Mourning Jewelry

The moment ended fast and it felt like a gunshot
wound to her chest. But she kept the bullet, wears
it around her neck as a reminder of that night, the
night when everything changed. He didn't even
give her a warning, just told her to leave, told her
that she wasn't worth the time, the effort, and that
made her angry. That pissed her off.

She didn't even know she shot him at first, not until
she was washing the blood off her hands, until
she was cleaning off the bullet that she ripped out of his
chest. It wasn't much, but it was the best memory
she had of him, so she kept it close, always above her
heart. And she got away with it, too, all the while talking to
the police with the bullet hanging in between her breasts.

MurderSex

I never meant for it to happen, and I certainly didn't mean to like it, but it felt good—like *really fucking good*—and then I couldn't stop. I wanted to do it every day: to see it, taste it, touch it, hear it. And *oh did I want to hear it.* The moans, the sighs, the screams. It was my heroine, my drug. And I needed it, craved it, and when I couldn't have it, the darkness set it. And then I took it anyway.

Naked for Neptune

There's a myth that Neptune brings the madness,
that it squashes every ounce of sanity left in a person's
mind and turns them on to every neurosis and mental
inhibition that lurks within the constructs of their imagination.
Knowing this, the young girl walked outside, naked and
dancing underneath the stars, screaming for the planet
to take her and give her the sight of schizophrenia, to instill
in her the depths of depression. She wanted sadness, craved
instability, and when the rain fell from the sky, she opened her
mouth and drank the tears of the night.

It moved within her
Ate her from the inside out

The girl screamed as insanity roamed down her throat,
as it filled her lungs, and swept her organs to the side. What
sweet music it made beneath her skin as it devoured the reality
she knew and replaced it with a new world, a new way of seeing;
one that bled the wounds of clairvoyance, that twisted and melted
matter into a surrealist orgy. Everything changed, and with it, so
did the girl. Her body moved with a sixth sense, a sixth feeling that
she couldn't unsee, couldn't undo, and when she walked back into
the house, when she put her clothes back on, there was a twinkle
in her eyes. A straitjacket around her heart.

Never Turn Off the Lights

The shadow women wait behind the wallpaper,
scratching off faux flowers as they dig their nails into
the plaster. I can hear them gossiping beneath the pillars
trying to lure me in, to kidnap me when the lights go out,
but I ignore their hisses, their whispers in the dark. They speak
to me of friendship, of an eternal sisterhood, but the hiccup
in their voices, the subtle hint of laughter in their tone, makes me
question their motives. No matter how bad I want to believe,
no matter how bad I want to join them, I won't turn off the lights.
I won't give in to their coven.

Nightingale

The bird sings to me,
it makes the scars go away, makes them fade. I hang
its cage in my bathroom, hang it right next to the mirror,
and before I put my makeup on in the morning, I pluck
one of its feathers and listen to it cry. Its voice soothes my
angry skin, erases the light pink bump that runs from my
eye to the tip of my lips, connecting the dots in serial killer
fashion. The louder the bird shrieks, the longer my
disfigurement stays away, and I want it to stay away, I want
the memories to stop, for the image of the knife to
stop replaying in my head, and I'd kill a thousand birds
if it meant I could stop seeing his face the second I close
my eyes. I'd cover myself in feathers, wash my face with
their blood if it meant I could go back to normal, if I meant
I no longer had to wear his signature on my skin for everyone
to see.

Nine Years, Nine Months

The dead women told me I would never know the feeling
of a full womb, that I was hollow, dried up, and barren,
a useless husk, a mockery of a woman. But they don't know
that I've grown to love that emptiness inside of me as if it were
my own. That I've nourished it, sheltered it, *protected* it, and
now it moves against my flesh, kicking out and screaming at night,
laughing at them as it grows, for our bond is much stronger
than that of a mother and child for misery takes nine years to
grow, and nine months to birth.

Obsession

I think thoughts that I shouldn't be thinking.
But then the thoughts aren't thoughts anymore,
and they become something else to think about,
something that I can't *stop* thinking about, because
the thoughts are bad. The thoughts are wrong.
the thoughts are thoughts that I shouldn't be thinking.
So I close my eyes and try to think about something else,
but I can't get that thought out of my head. But I think
I know how to now. I think I understand.

See in the beginning, I thought I had to deal with these
thoughts, that I'd have to constantly keep thinking, but
the thoughts grew. Became something that wasn't just in
my head. The thoughts that I'd been thinking were now the
actions that I'd been doing, and now that I'm doing and
not thinking, I don't have the thoughts. I don't have to think.
I can just do, and not worry.
I can just do and not think.

Open the Portal

It's a black carriage with tinted windows,
and it comes for her in the dark. She waits for
it outside her head, eyes closed as she leaves her
body behind, desperate to move on, anxious to
finally leave. She hears the horse neigh, hears it
click-clack, click-clack down the cobblestone
street, and when the faceless driver reaches out
her hand, the spirit girl accepts and rides into the
fog with the reaper, taking her chance with the
nameless chauffeur.

Orchids Take the Children

I planted a garden full of orchids and
covered my stomach in their petals at night,
praying that they'd fill me full of child. Years
passed and the orchids grew, never dying, only
getting stronger, taller. My little girl—my blessed,
sweet little girl—drawn to the pink, the vibrant hue
that lured her in and drank her up, ripped the flowers
from the ground and brought them inside as a present,
as an offering of love. But the orchids didn't love me,
the orchids loved her, and the little girl had tried to kill
them, had tried to remove them from their sacred
ground—their breeding ground—and so they took the
child to reassure that they'd never be removed again,
that they'd never be a threat to the children they were
responsible for bringing to life. There was only *real* mother
in our home, and she resided in the garden.

Oysters for the Grave

They buried her in pearls, but she wore them in her eyes
instead of around her neck. They put her in the ground,
six feet under with a blanket made of ash, and hoped that the
ground-up oyster shells would dry her out, get rid of her faster,
prevent her from ever coming back.

Pandora's Box

It wasn't curiosity that made her open the box;
it was a boy. And he promised her the heavens,
swore that she'd feel every pleasure, every joy
and every piece of excitement that the world
had to offer. He whispered in her ear, told her
about chance, about living for the moment—
in the moment—and Pandora liked the way he
talked, felt safe with his words, the verse that
rolled off his tongue and stole her breath with the
gentle flutter of a black bird's wings. She didn't
even have to think about it. Her mind was already
made up. Pandora ripped the antique key from her
necklace and unlocked the box, lifting the
lid slowly, carefully, until it was bent back and
open for everyone to see although there was
nothing but emptiness inside. Laughter filled the
forest as his voice crept inside her and pricked pins
and needles through her flesh. "You can't see evil,"
the boy said, kissing her on the lips, his tongue in her mouth,
pushing against her throat, her teeth, her lips. "Evil
is something you give in to, not something you
release." The boy took the box and threw it in the
lake, watching as the wet earth devoured the wooden
container. "Don't you know that giving into man is the
most dangerous sin of all?"

Peach-wood

Time wasn't an option; it simply wasn't there. The
girl didn't know what else to do but fall to her knees
and pray, to beg for protection from the men in the walls.
She reached into the corner and grabbed the peach-wood
staff—its energy moved within her, heightened her faith—
and she screamed at the entity, her lungs full of fear, her voice
cracking as the windows shattered and exploded in
fireworks of glass. The air grew cold in frigid whispers
as the glass hovered and spun, swarmed around her in sweeping
circles. The watchmen observed from the corner, waiting for the
moment, the split second when its defenses went down, and then
they rushed to the girl, to the peach-wood staff, and grabbed the
red lacquered stick and swung out at the demon, trapping it in the
bark. Its screams were loud and desperate as it fell through the
Gateway, but the watchmen didn't care. They knew their tigers
were hungry and that the virgin girl didn't deserve to die.

Piece Her Back Together Again

When she started to fall apart, no one really noticed because
it was the hidden parts that disappeared first: her love,
her empathy, her compassion. She stopped feeling, stopped
wanting altogether, and before she knew it, old emotions slid
off her skin like rain on metal roofing.

There wasn't a lot left to her after that, just skin and bone,
joints and muscles, until they, too, began to rot away. Her legs
decomposed from the waist down, her arms twisted and shriveled
into pale twigs that snapped off her torso and left scratch marks in
her play dough chest. Her mouth drooped at the sides and etched
itself into a permanent frown and she cried all day and all night,
wishing she could feel something, even if it was pain,
even if it was sadness, but nothing more than an encroaching
emptiness surrounded the room and hollowed her out, scraping
her clean by removing each and every part, burying her in a
sociopathic void.

Pluck Me

Feathers
are amputated
limbs
that fall off bodies—
The split-ends
of the corpse that
I weave into my braid
as I wave goodbye
to the bald body
I slaughtered
for the sake of
fashion

Quarantine the Dead

No matter the reason, the women came
for her in a stiletto stampede, stabbing her
heart with bad memories and leaving her for
dead in poor fashion. They hung her from the
ceiling with a horse-tail necklace and dressed
her in her antique wedding gown, all
white lace and half-eaten by moths. The girl
swung in the air without a fight and looked into
the hollow eyes that stared at her from below:
black, seedless eyes dipped in tar and burning with
hate. They were the eyes of her sisters, her mothers,
her aunts. And they wanted her, wanted her to pay,
to submit, to accept what she was and no matter how
hard she tried to lock them away,
to keep them from coming back, they finally did and they
did so in a family reunion so they could all watch
her pass and be the first to welcome her back into
the family she so readily turned her back on all
those years of witch burnings ago.

Quartz Begins the Initiation

They glittered in the sunlight like purple stars
dropped from the sky as they were placed in the young
girl's skin. It was her time—her birthright—to receive
the gift of sight and when the sun began to set, when it
dipped beneath the trees, her coven stripped her down and
laid her in the ground, force-feeding her orbs of quartz while
her sisters embedded them in her flesh. The rocks tasted like
hallucinations—soft, with a hint of lavender and a kick
of pine—and they opened her up, allowed her to blossom
like a ghost flower brought back to life. The girl's eyes rolled
to the back of her head, and the two white slits that took their
place watched the spirit world around her come to life. She saw
death, she saw life, and she watched it through a veil of violet as
the crystal lead her through her initiation and introduced her to a
new realm, a new sisterhood, one that would allow her to bridge the
natural and the spiritual world and unify the elements every time she
swallowed the stone.

Quietly, She Mourns

Like a coffin in the ground,
she sits and stills, making
her presence among the maggots,
taking her spot next to the
already-decomposed.

Ravens at Her Bedroom Window

Tap-tap-tap! Her black-bird children
wave hello with battered wings and
twisted feathers, their beaks pointed
and painted with blood and fur. They've
been hunting, eating away her nightmares
and now they've returned speckled in red,
dotted in good news. *Tap-tap-tap!* She opens
the window and invites her children in, and they
sit on her shoulders, and rest on her head,
not sleeping, but reading, studying her thoughts,
her dreams, her weaknesses, so they know who's
punishable, who's ready to be targeted next.

Razor's Edge

She picked up the razor, not because she wanted to die,
but because she wanted to live, and that shiny, thin,
sharp piece of metal would give her the ability to break through
the planes, to cut through the portal and open the Gateway to the
bridge where she could dance, and sing, and breathe, and live
amongst her own kind, amongst those that could see the fire,
hear the earth, taste the air, touch the water and feel the ether
around them.

Rest Among the Torches

The note was specific: "I found my way to magic,
through the fire of the earth. Keep me there in the
ashes, where I'll rise again." I know I should
have cremated her, that it was what she wanted,
that it was what she deserved, but how could I
let her go when she left me here, alone, without any
thought to how I would feel, how I would manage,
without her when she left? I tried to honor her—I really did—but
my heart broke every time I looked at her body, still
and lifeless on the forest floor, tied to the tree and
burned like a witch. She wanted the elements,
wanted the magic, and what else could I do but light
the world on fire and ensure that she stayed somewhere where
I knew she could never leave me again? I dug and I cried as
I marked her grave with torches and laid her to rest in the spot where
her blood stained the soil and her magic never came.

Room for Two

The bed sheets were cold and she couldn't sleep knowing that
the empty space next to her, the one with the slight indent in
the mattress and the smell of his cologne, held nothing but a
reminder of absence. She tossed and turned. Memories—there
were so many of them—all horrible, all vivid. The death rattle
in his throat, the choke at the end. He gagged his way to the reaper
and she had been there! She had watched him die in this very bed,
in this very spot!

She clutched the knife closer to her chest. Blood still stained the
tip from where she pushed it into his windpipe. She couldn't take
the thrashing, the constant movement. He was never still, and he
screamed—oh did he scream!—and so she stayed awake, eyes peeled
open from his shrieks. Eventually, she couldn't take it. She had to shut
him up, had to silence him. So she dug the knife in his throat, and severed
those heinous cords, slicing them apart piece by piece. But it didn't work,
didn't matter, because every time she closed her eyes, he still screamed,
this time louder, this time much worse.

Rosary Beads in Her Hair

She'd prayed daily—sometimes twice, maybe three times in a row—
and after the Our Fathers and the Hail Mary's she'd lay on the floor and
weep, hoping that her tears would cleanse her sins. Like gasoline, they
burned lines down her swollen and blistered cheeks for the Devil
had marked her, laid his hand on her face and singed the mark of a
temptress into the side of her head. It pulsed and seeped blood
when she spoke to the Lord, trying to beg for forgiveness when they all
knew that she wasn't sorry. She'd kneel down at the crucifix
and wrap her rosary beads in her hair, hoping that the blessed mother
would save her if she wore a crown of prayers, but the moment the stones
touched her flesh, they turned to ash and began to run down her face in the
blood river that seeped from the inverted cross in her scalp.

Set the World on Fire

If it's not fire,
if it's not all consuming...
I don't want it.

If it's not electric,
if it doesn't shock me...
I'm not interested.

And if it doesn't hurt,
if it doesn't make me think...
I'll walk away.

Because I want a love
that sets the world
on fire.

I want a love
that lights up
the night sky.

And if doesn't burn,
if the lightning doesn't strike,
then I'll wait...

Wait until the
ashes start to
fall.

Until the sparks
light me up
inside.

She's Worth the Chance of Death

Trust me. Take her hand and walk with her.
Just be careful. She might let you go.
She might let you *burn*. But she might keep you, too.

Sick and Twisted Affair

Dirty guilty come over quickly
I don't want to be alone tonight.
And I can't get the taste of you out of my mouth—
so I keep swallowing, keep remembering—letting your venom
string me along, letting it wake me up in the middle of the night,
craving, wanting, needing. I don't want to sit here and pretend,
don't want to close my eyes and imagine.
I want your toxins in my veins, the dirty little secrets that breed
between the sheets when everyone goes to bed. I want the late nights
and the early mornings, with no in-between, just body-to-body,
slick with sweat and no sense of time. Give me wrong and give me sin,
and I'll ride the Devil's laugh, hitch a ride to hell and enjoy
every last moment until we meet again, until the world blacks out
and everything starts to spin.

Sleeping Next to You

We were holed up in a hotel room, twisted in sheets
that fit like straitjackets. The room smelled like whiskey
and the taste of booze still sat hot on my tongue. I wanted
to scream, to pull myself out of your arms and crawl back
into the night, but I couldn't. Not after I crawled inside of you
and cried myself breathless.

The lamp flickered—on and off, off and on—and the movie
reel in my head clicked into place as I watched us dance,
drunk off the Devil's wine, and I smiled through the pain,
my lipstick smeared and the three o'clock hour telling all of
my secrets.

No part of me wanted to admit defeat, that I'd put down
my walls and let someone in. But I couldn't run anymore,
not with the comforter resting against your naked body,
tattooed and vulnerable, troubled by your own sins. Each
time we're together, I die a little more, but it's a murder that
I'm willing to turn a blind eye to. I'd gladly rip out my heart
and feed it to the moon if it meant another night with you, if
it meant another second on your lips, another moment spent
finding myself while I lie awake and explore.

I want to see angels and shake hands with demons and when
you touch me I see parts of Heaven, and all of Hell. My chest
fills with the sweetest delight, and crashes against the rocks that
surround my heart. I don't believe in love, but I believe in moments
like this, slices of life where two people connect and transcend the
here and now. What does it matter if one of us is dead if we can feel

the heat, the slap of body on body slick with sweat?
If we can combine our heartbeat and live—really live—
one night at a time, wouldn't the sweetest death be worth it
if we could do it together?

Slowly, He Lives

It's hard to properly mourn
when he won't go away. All
I want to do is wear my veil—
custom made with the lace from
my wedding dress, dyed the most
hurtful of blacks—but the bastard won't die
no matter how many times I try to kill him.

Succubus

Slow and steady like an arsenic drip,
he lays there intoxicated by the lullaby
that sings him to sleep. Her lips part in hunger,
eager to taste the flesh of man, and she pins him
like a dead butterfly, examining his body
as she spreads open his wings.

Her heart kisses his soul goodbye,
but not before it bathes in the
waters of lust. She licks at his lips,
tonguing at the growing desire brooding in an
unconscious mind as he gives himself
over to her—an unwilling participant in
love's final soliloquy.

Tears fall against pale skin
that glows in the shadows of the night, but
no emotion can sway the temptress,
for she *is* sin. An incarnate evil that feeds on
the union of bodies, watching for the very
moment when ecstasy takes over and she
can suck the carcass dry.

Sylvia

WHEN SHE FIRST MET SORROW, she was twenty-four. She hurt all the time and her chest felt swollen as if she swallowed a lead balloon. She was lost in a nightmare of depression. Her thoughts clouded in the aftermath of a thunder storm. Her eyes shut off from the light. She had been lost for some time. A wanderer who took the path less traveled because she knew she would be alone. Sylvia had forgotten how to feel, how to breathe. All she wanted was blackness. Blackness and silence.

She was laying in bed in three-day-old clothes when Sorrow swept her up in his arms like a dark prince sprung from the shadows. Cast in black, he cradled her like a broken doll. His words clinging to her like a wool blanket. His brown eyes whispered assurances as he brushed her hair with his fingers and held her as she cried. He was warm and inviting, and she burrowed into his chest taking refuge in his arms.

It felt good being with him.

It felt safe.

Sorrow was unlike any man she had ever met. He didn't ask why, nor did he judge her for her weakness. He merely accepted the sadness and stood by her as she battled her demons. He was no more and no less than Sylvia needed. Sorrow just was.

But then she met Pain.

Pain broke into her house when Sorrow went away. He filled her head with poison and brainwashed her comfort into madness. His eyes beat anger into her weary blues and when life seemed too much, he filled her thoughts with death.

Sylvia hated him. She cursed when he lay with her, and shrugged away at his touch. He was ice, and his voice made her cold. But Pain had something that Sorrow didn't. Pain had the ability to relate, and when they came together one night, there was no greater tragedy. Sylvia had found her partner in Pain. A soul that knew what it felt like to die but keep on living.

She saw Sorrow during the day, when the ache from her other half dug inside of her heart. She would curl up in his arms and sweat from the love that poured out of his flesh. He was humid and the heat made her crave frost. She didn't want someone that was trying to save her. She wanted someone to drown with.

Like Lazarus, she emerged from the darkness at night to meet her lover. Underneath the Yew Tree, they danced in the shadow of the moon, their bodies attached at the waist. Sylvia even smiled once, but always fell back into Sorrow's arms the next morning when the encroaching nothingness consumed her.

She did it because it felt like hell.

She did because it made her feel real.

Sylvia might have been in love with sorrow, but she would always be fucking pain.

Tag, You're it

Was it my turn to die?
Because I've lost track and I can't remember,
and I don't know anything anymore.
Everything's missing, gone, and there's nothing
but blackness, but stillness everywhere I look, and
when I reach out to grab you, you're smoke, fire, and
ash, and you crumble in the palm of my hand and leave
soot in my life-lines, my dead-lines.

I don't think it was my turn. I think you pushed
me into the darkness, but I'm not sure, and I can't
tell you how I feel because my heart isn't beating
and I don't know if I'm angry, if I'm sad, or
I'm just broken.

But I know you cheated me. That something
about this isn't right. That I'm not supposed
to be here, but I don't know how to go
back because I don't know where my body
is, where I left it—where you left it—and
the part of me that can think, that can try
to make a plan, knows that it's pointless. You
hid me from myself, locked me away with the cobwebs
and the maggots, and now I have nothing left to do
but search, but wander the world as a ghost
looking for her former corpse.

The Clock Strikes Scarlet

The storm raged in her eyes as she cried lightning,
sobbed thunder. Her tears were red and they stained
her face in crimson ovals that collected in the bags
that sat on her cheekbones.

Every night when dead hour arrived, she'd sense him,
maybe not fully, but partially, and that was enough for
her. She craved his presence even though it lasted only
a moment, a flutter in time as the stars froze in the
velvet sky.

And when the second hand stood still, and his outline
appeared, the wells in her chest overflowed and the
blood rain poured out her eyes. He stood amidst the fog,
blurred in a scarlet veil as she mourned her nightly suitor,
and choked on the scent of roses.

Death didn't claim him for he stood before her every night,
waiting, staring, but not trying to take her with him. Not once
did he reach out his hand, or beckon her forward, no matter
how much she begged, wished and prayed. Torn apart by a
pulse, they each lived in a type of Purgatory—twice damned
in life and death—ripped apart by a heartbeat and left to
weather the storm alone.

The Color Pink

It was Sunday,
and my color was pink—a soft blush on cheeks
that were half-frozen from the wind
who dipped me like a dance partner
and spun me in circles, my dress fanning out
and waving to him across the sidewalk.

I remember snowflakes
nestled in his auburn hair—he looked sad but yet
he'd never been more perfect to me than in that moment,
someone more than a lover, a star fallen from the sky
that landed in my arms, in my heart
but I knew I couldn't keep him.

When he turned to walk away
this time—I knew—for good,
I couldn't help but feel in my pockets
for some trick, some way to turn back time,
a time when that fallen star landed in my lap
and didn't burn out,
when the winter didn't leave scars
and my color didn't run
like watercolor down my cheeks.

Yet I don't mourn him
because for a brief moment—a day, a week, a year—
I held the galaxy in the palm of my hand
knowing that all stars are already dead,
but that they only shine for a select few.

The Day I Died

I REMEMBER THE DAY I lost my heart. I was young—too young, maybe—but the man told me it would be worth it, that falling in love—that dying—was well worth the pain. And I believed him. I wanted to feel *nothing*, to feel *everything*, and when I found myself locked in a hotel room, drinking away the absence as I sat in mounds of empty bottles and half-burned cigarettes, I knew that this was love. That this was what people talked about: the break, the agony, the split of power. Because when I fell in love, I lost myself. I became possessed, haunted by his smile, and now it's his face that forces me to wake up, to brush my hair, to put on my lipstick…

And so I died in his memory, more sure in that decision than in anything else I'd ever done in my life. I wanted to love even if it meant not getting it back in return. But I didn't know how—I was weak, innocent—I didn't know that the ache in my chest could actually hurt. And so I'd wake up in scratches, bleeding out on cheap carpet and covered in glass. The burns on my arms were in the shapes of teardrops, my throat raw from the screams. The furniture was broken and there were splinters in my feet. I tried to find him—looked behind doors, under beds, in the shower—but I couldn't. He wasn't there, and I started to think, to wonder, to feel, that maybe he never was. That maybe getting rid of my heart was a mistake. But when the man came back to me that night, holding regret in his hands, I said no.

Because I was in love. Shamelessly, painfully in love. And the misery was worth it. Was worth the casket as the bed, the poison in my cup, the demons in my dreams. It was better to feel to *nothing*, to feel *everything*, if it meant that at one point it wasn't fake. That at one point, it was real. That it had a shape, a purpose. That at one point, it had soul. So I walked away with my head held high and mascara smeared down my face. I wanted love, and I got it. It just wasn't what I bargained for.

The Night's Lover

The night covers her like a bruise,
black and blue, it colors her flesh in pain—
a dancing of lust and wrath—
she sinks in her body, trying to hide from
the clouds that stare at her in blurred judgment,
taking in her vulnerability,
breathing out her shame.

A slave to the darkness,
she knows she can't turn away its hands,
hands that have held her to the ground
since she was a girl, feeding her earth
and sadness, forcing her to dance
naked in the rain.

She opens her eyes to compliance,
takes in the scent of pine and fog,
lays down with her heart bleeding,
her legs open in surrender, her bones
broken and sore.

She knows her place, a shadow
amongst the shadows, but the bruising
does not lie. It reminds her of what happens
when she tries to run, to neglect her duties
to the darkness. A whore has choices,
but a slave will always wear its chains,
and hers are heavy with servitude.

The Primrose Path

Ophelia swam with flowers—
her heart broken in the
fallen petals of baby's breath
that lay tangled within
evergreen moss, sutured
inside her thick, blonde braid.

She smiled in her agony,
wearing pain like a crown
as the water filled up her lungs.
It turned her white dress
iridescent in the sunlight,
clinging to her flesh in fear
of separation. A child unwilling
to part with his mother.

She danced in the ripples—
a comfortable nymph
scorned by love,
yet free within the
floating glass that carried
her down through the forest,
and buried her amongst
the trees. A watery grave
for a woman that cried
herself to death.

The Women

Silhouettes line the hallway—
their shadows grow every night—
and I want to run,
but they follow me, chase me into nightmares
infiltrate my daydreams. These women—
and there are many—don't like the way
I scream at night, and they tell me to be quiet,
to keep my pain to myself, that they've witnessed
enough sadness to last them for centuries—and when I don't,
when I can't stop, they wrap my head in black cloth,
silence my cries with their funeral scarves
and hush me back to sleep, back to death, back to the wall
where my outline follows theirs, where my shadow
lives among theirs.

There are Voices in the Wind

A cold gust of autumn wind twirls her hair like
the whispers of dead children. *We're here, mother.*
We're always here. There's a softness to the way it
brushes through her, in her, around her with the delicacy
of wilted dandelions weighted down with fresh morning dew.
The chill of their kisses is one that she hasn't felt in years, not
since the fog—the gray maelstrom of forgotten yesterdays—stole
her babies all those harvests ago. She opens her arms and embraces
them, afraid that the voices, that the breeze, will stop
if she doesn't pay close attention, if she doesn't savor the way it
gently holds her hand or murmurs promises against her lips.

They Keep Dying

It doesn't matter what I do,
how I act,
or what I wear,
they die.
Every single one of them,
and they do it slow,
like wilting flowers
in the shadows
so I have to watch them wither,
watch them fall apart.
And I wonder if I'm being punished,
if I'm not supposed to love,
not supposed to be a wife.
Perhaps I was born to be a widow,
a woman destined for black,
because no matter the man,
no matter the boy,
he dies after the moment he
says 'I do.'

Ultraviolet Prayer

Hail Mary, light me up. There's a sickness in my veins. I've walked this life for a hundred years and I've swallowed the ashes, I've burned in the flames. I need something sharp, and I need something strong, so I pray to the virgin, I'll sing you your song. I need you to listen. I need you to see. I feel in love with a sinner, but he didn't fall for me. Now I'm down on my knees and I'm covered in shame, I scream out to God, I make love to his name. I need some forgiveness, I need to confess. Please send down the lightning. I ache to be blessed.

Until the Sun Comes Up

when you think of me, of we, of us,
I want you to think of storms and
how we rained on the city and drowned the night

of how we took to the streets
and survived off each other's lips
feeding like vampires as we ripped
apart bodies, fed like wolves

when you think of me, of us, of you
I want you to think of lightning and
how you struck me down, lit me up,
and left me alone to burn

Untitled

Existence is
mute—
A fleeting second
awakened
by a hiccup
in sleep.

Urns Make Me Drunk

It was silver and cold and I kept it in the cabinet
above the stove. No one needed to look at the urn,
and no one needed to know it was there—or that it was
empty—except me, especially in the evenings when I
made my seven o'clock cocktail and rubbed the rim
of my martini glass with his ashes instead of salt. I'd
throw the gin in the dead man's home, add some vermouth
and I'd shake it up, baby. Yeah, I'd shake it up, real good.

I kept his ashes in my fridge in a plastic bag that also
held my olives. I went and picked out a juicy one,
dropped it in my glass, and filled up my freedom drink
and sipped it slow, unable to hide the smile on my face. The
martinis tasted better now that he was dead, and I wasn't sure
if it was because of the ashes—the black glitter that gave it
it that extra kick—or the fact that he wasn't there to tell me
to stop drinking anymore.

Valley of Tears

There's a valley that holds the tears of little girls, and it soaks
them up like a paper towel made of dead leaves and brittle grass. I
hear it tastes like salt and bad decisions, and I wonder if it prefers
blondes, brunettes, or redheads.

Gulp.
Gulp.
Gulp.

I look at it sometimes and wonder how many sorrows it's consumed,
how many fears and bad memories, how many regrets, and then I wonder
if I go down there, if I sit on its tongue and tickle its tonsils, if it will just
swallow me whole so I can skip the crying.

Kill.
Kill.
Kill.

You know, people often get it wrong. It wasn't suicide that killed me,
it was the sadness, the loneliness. It just hurt too much to keep waking
up tired and when sounds started to hurt and the only pleasure I got
came from silence, that's when the valley called to me, and that's
when I ran to it in tears.

Die.
Die.
Die.

I thought it would hurt, but it didn't. I just kind of stopped existing, stopped being, when I jumped in its mouth and Death was wet and cold, and had teeth that bit me, but I didn't feel it. I was numb and I was invisible and I'd never been happier than in that moment when the valley stopped my heart.

Venus isn't Gentle

The goddess wears a costume of pearls and lets her wavy, blonde hair hang loose down her back. She smiles at men and bats her eyes, and she knows when she has them, knows when they've decided to submit to her every want and need, and she'll let them, but not as her equals. She'll only take them as her slaves, and when she takes off her clothes, when she removes her mask, there's nothing but serpents in her hair and poison in her eyes. She's not made of love but the goddess *is* made of passion, and she likes when her men scream, likes it when they cry. She drinks their tears for their youth and paints her lips red with their blood and when the men start to bore her, she fixes her dress and puts on her mask, and goes hunting for new lovers as the sea kisses the shore.

Vines are in Her Wardrobe

She often woke up strangled, choked half to death
by her nightgown made of vines, the ones that dug
into her skin and rubbed her belly raw. At first they
bothered her, but she'd gotten used to them now, and
when the stars came out to play, her babies would
wrap themselves around her, hug her full of thorns
and rock her to sleep, stealing her air until
she fell into a blue dream where flowers didn't grow
and twine threaded her lips.

Vows: Vicious Oral Whims of Speech

TEARS CREPT DOWN HER CHEEK like a slow death.

Seven years had passed and he still hadn't woken up.

Elizabeth circled his bed at a frantic pace and ran her hand against the cold, marble that had become his face. The lines around his eyes were smoothed over now as if he'd never laughed or cried a day in his life. She wondered what his eyes looked liked now. If they were glazed over and fighting death, or already snuffed out like a noir film at midnight. It shook her to think that she hadn't looked in his eyes for thousands of days. They were almost a memory.

"I, Matthew, take you Elizabeth, to be my wife," she whispered.

Her knees found the ground as the pain spread throughout her chest. She prayed it would kill her.

But no matter how much she prayed, it wasn't getting easier. Waking up was a herculean feat and there were times when she held her breath in hopes that God would think she was dead.

But God didn't listen to her.

God wasn't even there.

Elizabeth grabbed a fistful of the dirt blanket and felt it slide through her fingers like silk. For something that was supposed to provide warmth, it was frightfully cold. Chilled from the breath of disease that had coughed in her lover's face.

When he first became sick, she lived in a veil of denial. She mourned and went through the motions of a grieving wife, but not once did she think that fate would turn the death card. His hand was still warm that evening, and he fingered her wedding band as he drifted off to sleep. A sleep that held him captive and ever drowning in the blackness of his mind.

"To have and to hold from this day forward."

She leaned over and grabbed what was left of him.

He didn't even feel like Matthew. What was in her arms was a lie and it stabbed at her knowing that she would never get the real him back. She was stuck with this statue, this imposter of a man that did not know her touch, her kiss, her heart. He could not love her anymore, even though her heart knew nothing but him.

"For better or worse, for richer, for poorer, in sickness and in health."

Elizabeth pushed to her feet and wiped the dirt off from her tattered, white dress. It was already stained from yesterday's visit, and a fresh bout of tears mixed into the lace of her sweetheart neckline dampening the loose fabric. The tombstone reflected her grandmother's pearls as a fresh wave of despair spread through her body.

Everything hurt

And everything died.

She kissed his name and pretended to feel his lips, but they too were cold with the sting of death. Her arms slid around the gravestone and for a moment, she felt him. It never lasted long, but it was all she needed. Knowing that his spirit lingered was enough to keep her breathing. Enough to keep her alive.

"To love and to cherish from this day forward."

She repeated her vows every day when she visited the cemetery. But they were a lie.

"Till death do us part."

Wedding Ring

The ring bothered her, but only for a minute,
only for the amount of time it took for him to
walk across the room and catch her eye. And after
that, she didn't see it, and as far as she was concerned,
the ring wasn't even there to begin with.

So she laughed, flashed her charm, and smiled
a seductive grin—the one that sealed the deal
and guaranteed the night—and he followed her upstairs without
the slightest bit of hesitation, as if she were an angel
leading him to paradise.

Foolish man,
Predictable man

She ate him like candy, devoured his flesh without stopping,
and sucked on his bones as if they were made of sugar.
She consumed him in a way that no man would ever consume her,
and it was that taste of that dominance. That power, that filled her
with the gluttonous drive to feast on them, to make them pay for what they did,
what they thought they could get away with.
But the ring, it always made her sick,
so she stuck a finger down her throat and threw the blessed thing up,
rinsing away the taste of marriage in the bathroom sink.
The promise of monogamy
was the worst food poisoning of them all.

When the Only Hope is Sacrifice

Sometimes she wondered if she ever crossed his mind, if he ever thought about her the way she obsessed over him. And then there were the dreams. Did he see her when he closed his eyes, did he fantasize about her the way she touched herself over him? Was there a moment in the day when he craved her, when he yearned for her the way she desired him at nightfall, the way she wanted him at midnight? Sometimes she wondered if she ever hurt him the way he hurt her. If she ever broke his bones or slit open his wrists? If she ever forced him to drink away the madness, to pull the trigger as he screamed? Sometimes she wondered if dying for him was worth it, if sacrificing herself for him made him finally love her after all.

Where the Doomsday Song Hides

The music stopped when she cried for the sound of violins
and piano couldn't match the melodies dripping from her eyes,
the songs she wrote with her pain. They were ashamed to play
in her presence, embarrassed to compete with her compositions,
for she sobbed the key of anguish better than any musician extracting
an E-minor chord. Her muse was agony, her instrument its claws
on her heart, and when she warmed up in front of an audience,
they sat there—still, watching, waiting—ready for the clash of
sadness against sorrow. She came in strong, building a crescendo
as her wails filled up the stage. The dénouement. The climax.
She screamed as she fell, her chest open and convulsing to
the metronome's beat. Musicians couldn't look at her. The audience
turned away, and in the end, no one left. They just sat there, frozen
in their chairs—an ever present audience—dead from grief, slaughtered
from the siren's song.

White Night, Sleepless Night

Sleepless;
I wrap myself in bedsheets
cold as snow
in this white night that
blinds me,
even though my eyes are closed

I swallow the nightmares
drink away the dreams—
they come to me in pairs,
embracing me
like sisters often do

Restless;
I fluff the pillow
but it burst into tears,
trying to drown me,
to pull me under
even though I've already
stopped fighting

I lay in the blizzard,
catching snowflakes
on my tongue,
fantasizing about Sorrow
and when—no, if—
I can ever let him go

Xerox His Death Certificate

The man died and the girl could not have been happier. She ran to the hardware store and bought 500 nails and ran copies of his death certificate by the hundreds. She paid the cashier with three crisp hundred dollar bills and left the store skipping. It was the cheapest wallpaper she'd ever bought and she couldn't wait to hang the man all over the apartment. It would feel good to stab him again.

Yellow Makes Her Quiver

The sun peeks out from behind the ash-colored clouds
and the girl begins to shake. She doesn't like the way the
rays touch her face, and the yellow-orange-red dance that
the orb does in the sky makes her quiver. She fears if she
stays out here too long that it will burn away her halo and
show her for what she really is.

I won't let it take me
Not this time, not again

The girls hides in the shadows and prays for the clouds
to come back, wishing for another storm. There's something
safe about the blue-gray-white tango in the sky, but this
light ballet, this toss and turn of pastel happiness doesn't
sit well in her stomach. It makes her sick, makes her
horns start to bleed. If it stays like this much longer, she'll die
and she hates dying. It's her least favorite part of the day.

Yew-Berries, Yew-Tree

The funerary tree stood strong in the woods,
a sentinel waiting for the next threat, the next
person who would try to decapitate her head from
her body and use her wood—*her flesh!*—to make weapons
to cut down the rest of her brothers and sisters. But they
wouldn't take her, they wouldn't even see her coming and
she laughed, shaking her branches in the wind, and she cried,
dripping leaves down on the forest floor.

Berries spurted from her arms and she shook the red orbs off
her fingertips and spread them along the barren ground as blood
fruit for her enemies. Most of them were half-starved when they
got to her, she could see the hunger in their eyes, and the luscious
red and purple invitations were too hard to turn down.

Her bark face twisted into a smile as the men dropped one by one,
poisoned from the produce of her womb. They scratched at her,
called to her, but she couldn't hear them over the victory song her
family sang as they surrounded the huntsmen, eager to watch
them all die.

Yoke Necklace

She wore the yoke like a wooden choker and paraded around
the fields like royalty. Splinters dug into her throat, but
she didn't yank them out, didn't even wince. The girl just kept
moving, kept mowing through the meadow like a princess
wearing a tiara. And why shouldn't she? The girl was too young
to know she was a prisoner, too naïve to know she was trapped.

Zephyr's Unknown Wife

Gentlest of winds, he swept me off my feet with his infamous west-wind kiss and I fell through the clouds, head over heels, heels over head, waiting for him to take me back to his home in the sky and introduce me to my sisters, his dozen other wives, but they never got to know me, probably never knew I was there, for Zephyr kept me in cages, a bruised secret that the world could never hear, for I was his favorite and he wouldn't—couldn't—let the others know.

Zodiac Machine

She planned her pregnancies down to the day, made sure each of her children followed the stars and fell asleep with the planets. Twelve kids, twelve signs. She didn't think it would start the apocalypse, didn't think that the world would start to burn. But it did, and she smiled, and the Devil took her hand.

About the Author

Stephanie M. Wytovich is the Poetry Editor for Raw Dog Screaming Press, a book reviewer for *Nameless Magazine*, and a well-known coffee addict. She is a member of the Science Fiction Poetry Association and a graduate from Seton Hill University's MFA program for Writing Popular Fiction. Her poetry collection, *HYSTERIA*, is a Stoker Award finalist and can be found at www. rawdogscreaming.com. Follow Wytovich at stephaniewytovich.blogspot.com and on twitter @JustAfterSunset.